Baptis.
1006

Mo1

STORIES AND
BECKY MU

~Jrary

Living Waters Church
01803 552538
www.lwchurch.org.uk
Charity Reg: 1050312

Preston Baptist Church

Library

Mother Bumala
Stories and insight from the life of Becky Murray and One By One.
ISBN: 978-0-9928429-4-9

Published by Trywalla Publications on behalf of One By One
PO Box 762
Rotherham
S60 9JB
UK
Web: www.onebyone.net
E-mail: admin@onebyone.net

Words: Matthew Murray
Edited by: David Littlewood
Cover Design: Laura Murray
Cover Photo: Nick Jones

Printed in the United Kingdom. All rights reserved under International
Copyright Law. Contents and/or cover may not be reproduced in
whole or in part in any form without the express written consent of the
author/publisher.

<u>Dedication</u>

I want to dedicate this book to all my beautiful children. Firstly, to my own son, Josiah. You are the apple of my eye and bring so much joy to my heart.

And secondly, to all my King's kids in Kenya. You amaze me continually. I see Jesus in your eyes and I'm learning what it truly is to be a Christian by watching your examples. I am honoured to be called 'Momma' by these incredible children.

Contents

Preface

"Should I wait in your hotel room for you?" I wondered what nine-year-old Felicity could possibly mean. I'd found her begging on the streets of Bo, Sierra Leone, and was immediately drawn to help her.

She had no shoes, a problem I quickly rectified with the purchase of a pair of pretty pink sandals which cost less than £1. I then spent most of the day with Felicity, simply holding her hand, playing games with her and showing the kind of love she had clearly been missing in her short life.

But then came the dreaded question. Confused, I asked Felicity to repeat herself. "Should I wait in your hotel room for you?" she again mumbled. For a split second, I contemplated what she might have been suggesting. I'm a woman, she's a girl. She's nine. She couldn't possibly mean 'that', could she?

So I asked her a third time. Her final answer devastated me to the core. Sure enough, this precious, beautiful, innocent girl assumed that I'd bought her a pair of cheap shoes in return for sexual favours. She thought that in exchange for such a simple gift she would have to perform sexual acts on a woman almost three times her age.

My heart broke. How could a nine-year-old girl think this? What abuse must she have suffered to think this was normal? Had no one ever shown her true love? Shattered, emotional and angry, I managed to put on a brave face as I explained to Felicity why I'd bought her a pair of shoes. "Jesus loves you," I explained. "He has a plan for your life and wants to show you the true love of a Father."

I had to leave the next day, and I never saw little Felicity again. I often wonder what happened to her. Where did she go? Did she suffer more abuse? Has she found Christ now she is older?

I left Sierra Leone that week ruined. Something had changed in my heart. I knew I had to dedicate my life to helping children like Felicity. I might not be able to change the world, but I could change one person's world. And that was good enough for me…

Chapter 1 – A childlike faith

My infamous love for chocolate makes this story even more fascinating, but it also shows that God was birthing a passion for the poor in my heart even at a young age.

I can't remember the occasion – I was only four – but my mother tells me I was watching television one day while eating a chocolate biscuit. As the programme ended and the adverts began to run, a commercial showing needy African children appeared on the screen.

It was from a humanitarian charity that was appealing for funds to help the poor and destitute in the third world.

Even at the age of four, this touched my heart, and I apparently was quite upset. I put the chocolate biscuit on the table and told my mum that I didn't need it and to send it to Africa. She smiled, and explained that such a gesture wasn't possible, but she remembers the day clearly and believes the Holy Spirit was depositing a heart of compassion inside me.

A similar theme continued throughout my childhood. I'm also told that whenever my family took me to buy new toys, I'd always be drawn to the teddy bear in the unwanted pile, with its ear missing and eye patched up. I was more interested in these items than the more glamorous, expensive toys on offer.

A few years later, one of the men in my local church, Gerry Yates, was preaching about God's love. The previous week, he decided to put the congregation to the test by dressing up as a homeless man. He wore tatty clothes, dirtied his face so he was unrecognisable and appeared as

A childlike faith

needy and hurting as possible. Gerry sat at the back of the church, few people spoke to him and most in the room were scared and didn't really know how to treat him. I would have been about six or seven at the time, but I was touched with compassion for this man. How could he have become so poor? What could I do to help him?

I didn't have any money, but I went straight to the kitchen, asked one of the ladies who was serving for some sandwiches and a drink and carried them straight to Gerry. I thought this was the least I could do for our homeless visitor.

Mr Yates preached the following week and said that I was the only person who gave him any attention and treated him with genuine care.

He used it as an example that we should never ignore obvious needs around us, and that we

3

should always be looking for opportunities to showcase God's love. It was a simple yet profound message.

It's humbling to hear these stories years later, but I cannot for one minute take any credit for them. The Holy Spirit was clearly putting in me a heart of love for the poor and broken. It wasn't a natural emotion, but a call from Almighty God. A child cannot simply come up with these gestures and ideas, it has to be a work of the Holy Spirit.

This has taught me two things. Firstly, it is God who calls us. Although we stir up the gifts within us, He is the One who puts them there in the first place.

I describe this as the fingerprint of God. When He moulds and forms us in our mother's womb, He deposits something of Himself within us. The

Bible tells us that 'all good things come from above', so we must never take glory if God is gracious enough to use us.

Secondly, these stories show that the Lord can use anyone – it doesn't matter how old they are. God used me even as a small girl to speak to adults, and we should never discount the possibility that some of our greatest revelations might come through a child.

Many of the great principles and truths I have learned as a missionary have come about after meeting children, and it's a theme that's common throughout the Bible.

In John 6, a small boy shared his lunch with Jesus and thousands were fed; in 1 Samuel 3, God ignores the priest and begins to speak through the boy, Samuel. We all know the story of young

David, how he faced the giant in 1 Samuel 17 and defeated him with just a few stones.

As I've worked across Africa, I've seen young children lay their hands on sick bodies and see them healed. I've seen boys who have been abused and beaten by their parents go out onto the street and lead people to Christ. I've seen girls who are HIV positive pray, intercede and worship with such fervency and passion that the presence of God has filled the room where they were assembled.

We've taken teenagers with us on mission trips – for some it's been their first time out of their home country, yet God has used them in such powerful ways. They are fearless, brave and full of faith. They believe that the God they read about in the Bible is the God who is alive and moving in the nations today.

If God has put a thought, a dream, an idea or a plan into your heart, I encourage you to go for it – no matter how old you are. I'd also urge pastors and leaders to respect and honour the gift and calling of God on a young person's life. Of course we must be wise, and too much exposure and responsibility could crumble one so young, but isn't there a beauty in youthfulness?

I love what the Lord said to young Jeremiah: "Do not say, 'I am too young.' You must go to everyone I send you to and say whatever I command you."

I thank God for my childhood. I was raised in a wonderful, loving Christian home and my parents showed true love and joy. I thank God for their example.

Chapter 2 – The call of God

Although God had birthed in me a heart of
compassion at a young age, I never took the call of
God seriously until I was 18. I'd grown up in
church, attending every week with my family. I
was filled with the Holy Spirit, involved in all the
usual church activities such as worship teams and
youth groups, but I'd never truly surrendered my
life to Christ.

I went on my first mission trip to Sicily with a
group from my church which was led by my
pastor, John Andrews. John is an excellent Bible
teacher and was a wonderful pastor to me. He
taught me about mission and lived what he
preached. He regularly encouraged young people
to join him on mission trips across the world.

I preached my first sermon under John in Sicily and soon realised how much I enjoyed travelling and ministering overseas. I went to Sicily a second time and then signed up for the trip to Romania when I was 18.

At this point I was studying at college and had my heart set on becoming a lawyer. Although I was a committed Christian and loved serving the church and helping others, my real goal was to make lots of money, live in a big house, drive a nice car and climb the law ladder. But God had other ideas.

On the trip to Romania, it was the first time I'd worked with orphans. Simply showing these children the love of God and seeing their big beaming smiles gave me so much joy. During this trip, for probably the first time in my life, I heard the voice of God. He suddenly said to me: "Becky, one day you'll run your own children's home."

It was such a surprise, I really didn't know what to say or do. In fact, there was another girl on the trip whose name was Becky who had a passion to be a children's evangelist while I was pursuing my career dream. I joked and told God that he must have got the wrong Becky. That's how absurd and bizarre this message seemed.

People asked me how I knew it was God. In fact, this is a common question amongst Christians. How do I know it's God who has spoken to me? The answer is quite simple – you just know. It wasn't an audible call but an inner voice. It was as real as a human conversation. I knew without a shadow of doubt that God had told me that one day I would run my own orphanage. This was daunting, exciting and confusing. It wasn't something I'd been chasing or pursuing; I simply knew that God had spoken to me.

What do you do when you feel you have been given a call from God? That's another common question. Some well-meaning friends thought I should simply move to a foreign nation and start building an orphanage. That would have been unwise and potentially disastrous. Plus, I had no money. I knew that if God had called me He would pave the way and open the door in His perfect timing.

In the meantime, what should I do? I couldn't simply sit still. I wanted to show God that I was available, ready and willing. I determined that I would serve other ministries and other missionaries. It made sense to me that if I was to be a missionary, I needed to learn from others.

Shortly afterwards, one such man visited my local church to preach. His name was David Taylor, a former prisoner who God had radically saved and burdened with a calling to South America. David had moved to Colombia and was ministering to street children and those in extreme poverty there, so I registered for a one-month trip to help.

David and his ministry were wanting to buy computers for local schools, and I rather foolishly promised him that I would raise £2,000 towards the project. What a ridiculous promise to make. I had no money, no wealthy donors I could lean on for help and I needed a further £2,000 to pay for my flight, accommodation and expenses while in Colombia. What was I going to do?

But here I learned an important lesson about faith. God always supplies provision for His vision. His will = His bill! Through several fundraising initiatives and random donations from precious people in the church, I actually raised £5,000 as well as my money to get there. God had more than provided, and I learned that with God, anything is possible. This simple principle of committing to a project and trusting God for the finance afterwards has always stuck with me and has never let me down. Many times we want God to supply the money and then we will commit to the project, but faith works in reverse. We must step out so that God can step in. When he sees our faith, he always responds. Without faith, it's impossible to please Him.

I went to Colombia and had a fantastic four weeks there. I fell in love with the children, worked hard in the various projects and was offered a position to go there as a missionary. This was so tempting and, naturally speaking, made perfect sense. God had burdened me with a heart for missions and a passion for children. Here was an opportunity to outwork that within a good, established ministry.

But something inside me knew it wouldn't have been right to accept the offer. God had something else in store, but what was it?

Chapter 3 – An encounter with God

My pastor Peter Morris' son Nathan had recently recommitted his life to Christ after years of rebellion. Nathan was an all or nothing kind of guy, and it was clear that God had touched him in a powerful way when he came back to church. He had started evangelising on the streets of Cambridge where he lived, but moved back to the church my family had started attending in the small village of Wath-Upon-Dearne, near Rotherham in South Yorkshire. Nathan hadn't been a Christian for long, but he started holding Saturday night services which would last for hours. People would travel from all across the country to experience the unique move of the Holy Spirit that was taking place there.

During this time, I attended some of the meetings, but was quite unsure of their authenticity. People would fall on the floor and sometimes stay there for hours, others would groan, shake and make strange noises and there were other manifestations that didn't at all seem godly or biblical to me. However, despite my reservations, I struck up a good friendship with Nathan and despite my questions about the manifestations in his meetings, there was no doubt that God was using him in a wonderful way.

Pastor Peter, his wife Pam and Nathan were taking a group from the church to America for a mission trip. I decided to join them, and on the journey there Nathan and I spent hours talking about Jesus. Although I was baptised in the Holy Spirit and was a committed Pentecostal girl who spoke in tongues and served the church well, I had to confess that Nathan had something in his life that I didn't. He talked of an intimacy with Jesus that I didn't possess and burned with a fire that I knew was missing from my Christian walk. This made me hungry and desperate for God. I knew I needed more.

During the vacation, we made the long drive to Brownsville Assemblies of God in Pensacola, Florida, to a church that had been experiencing revival for many years. Millions had gone through the church's doors and thousands were saved after a visitation of the Holy Spirit on Father's Day 1995. I was slightly nervous about going there. No doubt people would be falling on the floor and shaking – a phenomenon I wasn't particularly keen on – and as I knew the rest of our group loved these kind of meetings, my primary concern was that I'd be the odd one out.

We arrived at Brownsville and my concerns only deepened. Tommy Tenney preached a good message but sure enough, some of the strange manifestations that I'd doubted were beginning to take place.

After the service, we were gathered outside the building ready to get into our minibus when suddenly a group led by Bible teacher Dr Sandy Kirk wandered over and asked if they could pray for us in the car park. I thought it was a bit strange to pray outside the building, but my fears only increased when I noticed one of the team was a woman whose head was shaking in a way that I disagreed with.

Several of our team were prayed for and fell on the floor, and then this lady – who I later found out to be named Mary Clay – started praying for me. I wanted to remain polite and respectful so allowed her to do so, but what happened next came as a complete shock.

Mary put her hand on my head and I instantly collapsed to the floor. My whole body became uncontrollable and I had no idea what was happening. I couldn't stand to my feet and couldn't speak any coherent English. This experience lasted for almost one hour. My pastor and some of the men on the team had to pick me up and literally slide me into the vehicle. Then, through absolutely no choice of my own, I started to make some of the same noises that I'd previously criticised. It was a groaning that couldn't be explained, an inner burden and desire for God. All I could do was utter the words 'It's real, it's real, it's real'. These words kept coming out of my mouth as tears trickled down my face.

At one point I honestly thought I'd had a stroke. My hands were twisted, my body was out of control and I couldn't function like a normal person. What on earth was happening?

On reflection later that evening, I knew that God had touched me. For the first time in my life I'd encountered His presence in such a real and powerful way. How could I ever be the same again? This was that which Nathan had been talking about. This was the intimacy with God that I'd desired. I'd previously put God in a box and thought I could dictate how He moved, but my theology was challenged in an instant. From now on, God wouldn't just be my master, my boss and my ruler, but He'd be my friend, my father and the lover of my soul. He'd touched me with His presence and allowed me into a whole new world that I didn't even know existed. I was His child, and my life would never be the same again.

This showed me that there are different levels of intimacy with God. Yes, I was born again and filled with the Holy Spirit, but for the first time in my life I felt like I truly knew Him. Not everyone will have an experience like I described, and such physical manifestations should never be our focus, but there's no denying that God touched me in that church car park. It was a life-defining moment and one I will be eternally grateful for.

Having returned from America, my passion for missions and the nations only increased. One of my inspirations and heroes was a preacher named Heidi Baker, who has planted thousands of orphanages and churches across the world. She is one of the great missionaries of our generation and I applied to join her school of ministry for a three-month internship in Mozambique. I decided to leave my well-paid and secure job almost instantly,

I packed up a suitcase and caught four planes before landing in Pemba, Mozambique.

Although I went to Africa hoping to give, impart and pour out, God had very different ideas. It was during this three-month stint that my relationship with Christ deepened to a further level. I would spend hours in His presence, worshipping, praying and being still, learning to listen to His voice and having intimacy with Him. It was the most valuable period of my entire Christian life. I learned about the importance of spending time with Jesus. If I could learn to be intimate with God and to hear His voice, I knew that everything else would soon follow.

Chapter 4 – Shaking nations

As my love for God grew, so did my love for others. You could say that the two go hand in hand. The more we love our Saviour, the more we want others to experience that same joy. It was while I was in Mozambique that I felt God speak to me to train to be a nurse. He showed me Ezekiel 47:12, where the Lord gives the prophet a vision of a river where there would be 'fruit for food and leaves for medicine'. As clear as anything, I knew God was telling me to go back to school to study nursing. I was met with slight opposition from people close to me who thought I was making the wrong decision. But God's favour was revealed when I applied for the course and was granted a place with no tuition fees, as well as a generous cash allowance each month for my living expenses. The university I attended stopped this funding after my my year group's applications, and I later discovered that I was the last applicant in my year to receive it. This further confirmed I was on the right track and I knew my training would undoubtedly help me in third world nations where medical needs were extreme.

At the same time, God was beginning to further use Nathan Morris in our home church in Yorkshire, and he had officially launched his ministry, Shake The Nations, when he was invited to Sierra Leone in April 2006 to hold a series of gospel crusades throughout the country. Nathan asked me to join him and to run several aid projects in conjunction with the crusades, and Shake The Nations One By One, the humanitarian arm of Nathan's ministry, was duly formed.

It was on this trip that I first worked alongside my future husband, Matthew – although it was far from love at first sight! Matthew had only been a Christian for just over a year, after finding Christ in a Nathan Morris Saturday night revival meeting. He had subsequently become best friends with Nathan and was now his personal assistant and crusade co-ordinator. Matthew had printed about 10,000 decision cards and asked our team members to fit them in their already-packed suitcases, whereas I had many items of clothing for the poor which had been donated and I asked the team to do the same. Team members were reluctant to take either the decision cards or the clothing items due to a lack of space in their suitcases, and Matthew and I were at instant loggerheads and both were quite stubborn about which was more important. Matthew insisted that following-up new converts should take priority, but my concern was for the poor children who had no clothes. In the end, neither of us won and we both had to take less items than we'd hoped for.

Most of the team members on the trip to Sierra Leone were married couples, other than myself and Matthew, so when it came to praying together in the crusade, we had no choice but to pair-up. This annoyed both of us, as we couldn't stand the sight of each other. However, despite the initial anguish, God turned the situation around. As Matthew and I prayed for the sick, they began to get healed. He also made me laugh and I figured he couldn't be such a bad guy if people were being healed as he laid hands on them. This was the beginning of our friendship, and although we didn't start dating until later that year, we eventually married in 2008. Nathan was best man at our wedding, his father Peter conducted the ceremony and Bishop Abu Koroma, from Sierra Leone, flew in to preach at our wedding. It was an extremely humble and low-key ceremony, but I'd married my soul-mate and that's all that mattered.

Matthew has been a great supporter of me ever since that first Sierra Leone trip, and there's no one else who I'd want to share my life with. He loves God, he's great with people and has a passion for missions and evangelism. He is brilliant at making ideas and dreams come to pass, and rarely takes no for an answer! I'd like to think we make a great team and complement each other, which is vital for married couples serious about ministry.

Matthew and I served Nathan and Shake The Nations for several years. Matthew spent almost every day of his life for five years with Nathan, and he would often be up until the early hours of the morning sending e-mails, making phone calls and working as hard as he could to ensure Shake

The Nations was ran with excellence and efficiency.

I must say that working alongside Nathan Morris was a great privilege. I consider Nathan a brother in Christ. He is not only a powerful and anointed preacher but is exactly the same away from the pulpit too. He knows how to have a good laugh and was always a great encouragement to me in my first trips to Africa. He pushed me out of my comfort zone and trusted me with his ministry's humanitarian department. He believed in me throughout those early years, and I'll always be grateful to him for that.

It's also worth mentioning that although I was responsible for the humanitarian work in Shake The Nations, I always attended Nathan's crusades and enjoyed being a part of his ministry team. We would pray for the sick every night and saw some wonderful miracles. The blind, deaf and lame were healed in every crusade and each trip was filled with such incredible reports and fantastic testimonies. I don't have space to go into details of some of the great stories of Shake The Nations, but being part of such a frontline evangelistic ministry raised my faith and showed me that God wants to heal his people. All we have to do is pray for them. It really is that simple.

Chapter 5 – Food for thought

Our first trip to Sierra Leone couldn't have started any worse. After a long flight, a ferry journey and a lengthy drive on bumpy roads, our car broke down as we travelled to the town of Kenema. The other vehicles had gone on ahead of us and we were stranded in the middle of nowhere, and it was getting dark. There was an electrical fault with the vehicle and the driver said that a rare part was missing which could take hours to arrive. I don't really get scared, but when the driver got worried, I got worried. We were stuck in the back-end of Africa, needing a tiny electrical part to fix our car and night-time was fast approaching.

As the team panicked and wondered what might happen to them, a man suddenly approached us on a bicycle. He rode past us, stopped and asked what the problem was. We explained what had happened to our car and he smiled, reached into a small basket at the front of his bike and pulled out this mystery electrical item. We couldn't believe what was happening. Furthermore, he agreed to fit it for free – a miracle itself in Sierra Leone!

He fixed the car and rode off into the night. We thanked God and our driver continued on the journey to Kenema. On reflection, this is one of the most incredible miracles I've ever witnessed. What are the chances of a man carrying such an obscure mechanical part? I'm not going to say he was an angel, but I'm certainly not going to say he wasn't. This incident showed me that God always looks after His servants when they are on His mission field. How comforting.

I could write an entire book on my time in Sierra Leone. It truly is a nation that is close to my heart. We met children whose families had been devastated by the civil war. Rebels would break into homes and ask children if their father would like a 'long sleeve or a short sleeve'. The child's answer would determine if the rebels cut off the father's arm at the elbow or wrist. The affects of this war are horrendous, and the poverty and strife still continues in Sierra Leone long after the war has finished.

In the town of Bo, my friend Amanda Marrow and I came across two children who were begging on the streets. One was a young boy named Solomon, the other a nine-year-old girl named Felicity. Their stories broke our hearts, as they told how they had been abandoned and thrown out, having to fend for themselves and having no proper education. We showed them the love of God in a very simple way – giving them clothes, sweets and just playing with them – something they'd been robbed of in their short, tragic lives. The words of Felicity will stay with me forever. As we were leaving to go to the evening's crusade, she asked me: "Should I wait in your hotel room for you?" I didn't understand what she meant, but on further quizzing, this poor girl thought that I'd bought her a pair of shoes in return for sexual favours. That's how devastating and heartbreaking the situation in Sierra Leone is. Her words tore my heart in two. I was messed up. Life shouldn't be like this for anyone, let alone a small child. What must she have gone through to even think that of an older woman? That night, we took Solomon and Felicity to the gospel crusade and they saw a blind man who begged on the same street as them be healed during the meeting. It was fascinating to see the children's faces as they witnessed miracles and God's presence for the first time.

As we visited several orphanages and centres throughout Sierra Leone, I began to preach about the little boy in the Gospels who turned up with his loaves and fishes which eventually fed 5,000. I taught how if we give God the small, He can turn it into something big. Little did I know that I was preaching to myself. The following day, we were in a disabled centre in Freetown, a rundown place with some extremely needy amputees.

We had a box full of food to feed 50 people but to our shock, 100 showed up. This was worrying. You don't want to run out of food in Africa, or you could seriously have a riot on your hands. As we continued to serve the rice and beans, I kept praying. Amazingly, everyone ate. Prior to leaving, a lady arrived with a large washing bowl and asked if she could take any leftovers to a nearby family who were too ill to attend the feeding programme.

We scraped the remaining food into the washing bowl but were staggered to see that the leftovers now appeared larger than the food we began with. There's no doubt in my mind that God multiplied the food. Not only did 100 people eat – double what we had prepared for – but the leftovers were larger than our original portion. What a mighty God we serve!

The following day, our faith was put to the test again as we visited a local school. We had the same box to feed 50 but this time, almost 200 turned up. Again, we served and prayed, although this time, I must confess I had my doubts as to whether we could feed everyone. I'm a big believer that if you're feeding the poor, you must give a generous portion, but on three occasions, one of the volunteers told us that we must reduce our portion sizes as the food was going to run out.

On the first two occasions, I was adamant that there'd be enough, but by the third time, I could see the rice running out and a long line of people were still waiting for their meal. I almost buckled at this point, but turned to my left and there was Amanda who simply nodded. That was enough to say she was with me – and that's all I needed. We believed God together, every single person ate a full portion and incredibly, there were twelve plates left over – just like at the feeding of the 5,000. Amanda is the kind of person who would never get up and preach in front of a crowd, yet without her faith that day, I don't believe that miracle would have happened. Ministry is never about one person, but we're an army together, united for the battle ahead.

We returned to Sierra Leone the following year and again held gospel crusades and ministered to the poor. This time we hosted a children's crusade, and were well prepared, or so we thought, as we arrived with enough food to feed 500. Amazingly, however, 2,000 kids showed up but again God performed a miracle and each child ate.

Chapter 6 – A brothel and a mosque

The light of the gospel shines brightest in the darkest places, and we saw this in action regularly during the days of Shake The Nations One By One.

In Sierra Leone in 2007, our team was travelling around villages distributing rice and preaching the gospel in open air when we came to one place that was a Muslim-dominated region. The main focal point in the village was the local mosque, so I decided to climb up the steps, gather a crowd and began to preach about Jesus. The reaction was so positive that I began to question my interpreter and doubted whether he was repeating the correct words, so I shouted: "Jesus is the one and true living God." The interpreter repeated these words and the small crowd began to clap and cheer. Several responded to the gospel that day. What a glorious Saviour we have.

In 2008 we visited Lagos, Nigeria, and my dear friend Toyin Kamgaing asked me to visit a brothel – this was a first! Toyin linked me to her friend Lorraine Nzimiro, who was granted access to minister to working girls and give them a second chance at life. I wondered what on earth I could preach about, but the Holy Spirit helped me out. The previous night, I was laid in my hotel room bed when the voice of the Lord spoke to me: "These girls cannot be bought at a price by any man, I have already paid the ultimate price in sending my son Jesus to die for them." Wow, God had given me a message, and my nerves turned to excitement as I began to contemplate what God was going to do.

The brothel was more like a bar, with bedrooms adjoining. The girls gathered in the bar and men would have a drink there before deciding which girl they wanted to sleep with. To my shock, when I arrived, not only were the girls there but the men were gathered at the other side. Now I was really out of my comfort zone and began to sense immediate danger. I turned my back to the men and faced the women, sharing with them about God's love and the message the Lord had given me the previous night. But halfway through my sermon, the Holy Spirit spoke to me. "Didn't I die for the men as well?" he said. This convicted me immediately. There I was preaching about the love of Christ but I had my back turned to the men who I had completely judged and condemned in my mind. I took a step back and preached the word of God to everyone in the room.

As I came to the end of my message, I appealed for those who wanted to become Christians to respond. Every woman in the room put up their hand and said they wanted to receive Jesus, and amazingly, some of the men did too. One man, a Muslim, came up to Toyin afterwards and said that he had never visited a brothel in his life, but that day he felt drawn in. After hearing the gospel, he suddenly knew why. Lorraine has continued her ministry in the Nigerian brothels, and has seen many girls rescued from evil environments and given jobs.

On that same trip to Nigeria, Shake The Nations accompanied Reinhard Bonnke on one of his historically huge gospel crusades. This was a great privilege. We stayed in the same hotel as Reinhard, ate with him at meal times and listened as he shared stories of his time on the mission field. I honour Evangelist Bonnke for what he has done for the continent of Africa. It was a delight to meet him and spend valuable time in his presence.

We also visited India on our travels, and prior to our visit, my friend Amanda Marrow felt God speak to her about widows whilst I had felt burdened to buy sewing machines. I approached Pastor David Prakasam, who we were working with in the city of Coimbatore, and he said that they were opening a widow's centre that very week. This was immediate confirmation for me that God wanted us to step in, so we bought the women sewing machines which enabled them to earn money and get their lives back on track. Pastor Prakasam said this became the blueprint for his ministry and they have helped many women since our initial visit.

On a trip to Tanzania in 2008 we saw the protection of God in a great way. My friend Charlotte Seymour and I had wandered off into an extremely poor village near the capital city, Dar es

Salaam. We had a large group of children
following us as we continued to walk, but we came
across a man on a sewing machine who, in perfect
English, warned us that if we went any further a
group of drunk men would rape and kill us. We
quickly turned around and ran for our lives.
Normally, if someone in a remote village speaks
English, it means they've had a good education,
whereas a tailor on a sewing machine would be
uneducated and would only speak in a local dialect.
It was an unusual incident and again I refuse to
rule out the possibility that we were entertaining an
angel that afternoon.

Another memory that will stay with me forever is
when we went to a remote village near Bo, Sierra
Leone, in 2009. I was with my friend Pearlcya
Sakayam and we were distributing rice and
charitable items. A man who had been in Nathan

Morris' crusade had returned to the village with reports of miracles and salvation, but his fellow villagers thought he was lying. Soon afterwards, however, we arrived and a crowd quickly gathered, intrigued by the white faces and the miracle reports. I began to preach the gospel in a bamboo-sheltered bus stop and I'll never forget the reaction of the people. As I described the crucifixion and resurrection of Christ, the crowd began to weep, shout for joy and sing songs of celebration. They had never heard these precious, life-saving words before. I had to shout loud above their tears as the words of the gospel pierced their hearts. Spontaneous worship flowed from brand new converts who had no concept of church and religion.

I'm forever amazed at the power of the Christian message. Although the stated aim of our charity is to meet practical needs such as food and clothing, we also make it a priority to preach the gospel. It truly is the power of God unto salvation and the only hope for the nations of the world.

Chapter 7 – Bumala 'B

More than a decade had gone by since God had told me I'd run my own orphanage, and a few well-meaning friends were beginning to have their doubts. "If God's told you, why don't you just go and do it?" they would say. I understood what they were meaning.

There's an element of the call of God where you simply have to 'go', but there's also an art in patience, trust and God's perfect timing.

In the Bible we read of Abraham and Sarah, who were desperate for a child. Before Abraham had his promised son, Isaac, he had another son, Ishmael. This wasn't the son God had planned for him, but he went and did his own thing anyway. In the same manner, I didn't want to do anything out of God's will; I was willing to wait for my Isaac.

By 2009 I'd travelled extensively with Shake The Nations and was also studying to be a nurse as well as being newly married to Matthew. We had a trip to Kenya coming up and I was praying about it and asking the Lord what I should do. Then, just as clearly as God spoke to me in Romania when I was 18 about running a children's home, he whispered again: "Now's the time, look for land." This filled with me immediate excitement. My dream was going to be a reality. Of course all I had was a word from God, but that was really all I needed. I flew to Kenya, ready for the next stage of my ministry.

Nathan, Matthew and the other Shake The Nations team members who had previously visited Kenya spoke highly of the nation. Matthew loved it so much that we went there for our honeymoon in

2008, and being an African fanatic myself, I certainly wasn't going to argue.

While we were on our honeymoon, Pastor Gerald Okoth, the man who organised the crusades for Nathan, drove through the night (almost 20 hours in total), so that he could spend a day with us. He immediately impressed me as a man of integrity and I promised him I would join Nathan and Matthew on their next crusade in Kenya.

Pastor Gerald was born in a village close to the Uganda border named Bumala 'B. It's a remote village, with no shops or market place for about 20 miles. There was no church there and no missionary or evangelist had ever visited – until Shake The Nations' first crusade there in November 2006. I wasn't there to witness that meeting, but Nathan, Matthew and the team that went believe it was the greatest move of God they had ever witnessed. They saw thousands saved, many miracles and a church was planted as a result of the crusade. Such was the prominence of the meeting, local history books now record what God did.

Fast forward three years, and here we were going to Busia, the closest city to Bumala 'B, to hold a gospel crusade. A team from America had joined our group from England, and a few hours after we had gathered, I met with Pastor Gerald and shared with him that God had spoken to me to look for land. As I spoke, his eyes lit up and he smiled, telling me that he'd been given a few acres of land that very week and his lifelong passion had been to build an orphanage in his home village. The need was great, he said. There were many orphans, children who were HIV positive, others had been abandoned by their parents, and poverty in the region was extreme with families struggling to feed their children and buy them clothes. Gerald, a highly-trained and experienced accountant for Kenya's second largest sugar firm, didn't have the resources or the manpower to make his dream come to pass and had been praying for God to send him someone to assist him. How wonderful that God spoke to me at the same time.

Pastor Gerald and I prayed and agreed we would join forces to build a children's home in Bumala 'B. I visited there on the Sunday, spending just a few hours in the tin church that Shake The Nations had planted in 2006. I loved the village immediately and knew it was the kind of place God would send me to. It was remote Africa, exactly where my heart was. I was like a kid at Christmas, excited at all what was to come.

Of course one thing I didn't realise on that hot November afternoon was the financial magnitude of what we were about to take on. Shake The Nations One By One had a mere £1,000 in its bank account. We were a tiny department of a small crusade ministry. Our resources were limited, but we knew our God was limitless, so we went ahead in faith.

A few months later, Pastor Gerald had hired some architects and the plans were drawn up. The three-storey building, which could house up to 100 children and included a primary school, would cost £110,000. This was cheap by Western standards, but it was still a humongous amount. I believe in fundraising. In fact, we receive many precious donations from people who complete marathons, climb mountains and bake cakes for our work in the nations. I'm grateful to them, but I knew that to achieve this dream, I would need more than a team of committed fundraisers. I handed Pastor Gerald the £1,000 from our bank account, knowing that now I had nothing. If this home was to open, God would have to perform a miracle.

Children respond to the gospel in Sierra Leone (2007).

Some of the beautiful boys and girls in Bo, Sierra Leone.

*Solomon and Felicity, the first children ever helped by One By One,
along with my dear friend Amanda Marrow.*

*Praying for a blind widow in India (2009).
What a privilege to pray for the sick.*

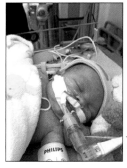

My precious son Josiah was so sick when he was first born. Here he is on a life support machine in Sheffield Children's Hospital.

Fit and well: Matthew and Josiah on a family photo-shoot as Josiah's health continued to improve.

Pastor Gerald Okoth and I go through the architect's drawings for King's Children's Home.

Opening ceremony: Pastor Gerald and I join local dignitaries in opening King's Children's Home.

The stunning King's Children's Home. I love this building every time I see it.

Baptising some of our King's children in a local river. What a joy to see them accept Jesus.

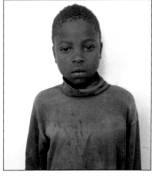

Nine-year-old David Zakayo was found in a house full of worms and insects. He had been living alone and fending for himself for four years.

David today. He is now in King's Children's Home. His life has been completely transformed by the love of Jesus.

Little Mohammed's feet were infested by jiggers, a parasite that eats away at the flesh.

After medical care, Mohammed's feet are now in perfect condition.

King's Children's Home and its 105 children in 2014.

Chapter 8 – The Bay of the Holy Spirit

"This feels like Father's Day, 1995," shouted Pastor John Kilpatrick as miracles, signs and wonders began to break out at the Open Heavens Conference at Church of His Presence in Mobile, Alabama, on July 23, 2010. Pastor Kilpatrick had previously led the Brownsville Revival – where my life had been changed – and if anyone recognised a move of God, it was him. He said the atmosphere that night was identical to the day the Brownsville Revival started. We knew God had something big in store.

Nathan Morris was the guest speaker that night and Matthew and I were there alongside him. What was meant to be a two-day conference turned into a nine-month revival, as thousands travelled from across the world to witness what God was doing. There were many incredible miracles and the revival was broadcast throughout the world as GOD TV sent in their cameras and filmed the meetings each night.

I'd describe my time at the Bay of the Holy Spirit – the original name that Spanish explorers gave Mobile Bay – as the most exciting yet frustrating period of my life. I had recently completed my nurse training and started working in my local hospital in England, but when the revival broke out that night I knew life would never be the same again. I returned home to England for five weeks – leaving Matthew in Alabama – and quit my job as a nurse. It was a bizarre feeling, but I had no choice but to serve alongside my husband. Moreover, I was also excited to be a part of this move of God.

I was given a job working as a receptionist at Church of His Presence for Pastor Kilpatrick. I would answer the phones, liaise with visitors and follow-up testimonies. The Bay Revival, as it became known, was renowned for its signs and wonders, and we truly did see remarkable miracles every night. The most famous healing was that of Delia Knox, a worship leader who was paralysed from the waist down after a car accident some 22 years earlier. After attending the Bay Revival, she was completely healed, and returned frequently to the church to tell her story. A little boy named Caleb attended with a brain tumour and had the medical scans to prove it. He returned a few weeks later showing new scans that revealed the tumour had miraculously vanished. Miracles like this were frequent and would be worth an entire book in their own right.

As I followed up many of these great testimonies, one thing that impressed me was the authenticity and integrity of the miracles. Of course we'd seen similar healings in Africa, but due to the lack of health care and finance to pay for check-ups in nations like Sierra Leone, many of the miracles in the gospel crusades were never verified medically. It was different in America, however, as we were able to obtain many letters from doctors, reports and scans proving that people had been genuinely healed.

It was quite surreal to be a part of such a high-profile move of God. Matthew was Nathan's right-hand man and would read out testimonies on his iPad every night of what the Lord had done. I must say that the people of America were hospitable, warm, friendly and devoted to God. We loved our time in Alabama. Church of His Presence and Pastor Kilpatrick will always be special to us – they welcomed us as family and we were privileged to play just a small part in what God was doing.

In the midst of this nine-month stint in America, my children's home dream was put to one side. All fundraising attempts were postponed and we gave our entire lives to serving Nathan at the Bay Revival. This wasn't easy. My heart was longing for Africa and I knew that these precious babies there needed me. But there was no denying that God was moving in Alabama and I had to serve God by supporting both Nathan and my husband Matthew. I learned a valuable lesson there. We must always be willing to serve others and lay down our own ambitions and plans.

Matthew and I had saved hard for a new house and had only been in it for three weeks when the Bay Revival started. We left that house empty for almost one year, which some people thought was absurd. But we trusted God, submitted our plans to Him and knew that His ultimate plan would be revealed. Also, I knew beyond a shadow of doubt that the children's home would happen – God had said so. I just had to be patient, which, at the time, wasn't easy.

I was worshipping one night at the Bay Revival when I felt God tell me to step outside of the auditorium. This seemed strange, as the meeting was going on inside, but I obeyed, walked out and looked across the beautiful bay. Immediately, a huge ship began to sail past. On it were the words 'Overseas Rebecca'. At first the ship was moving extremely slowly, but as it approached me, it gathered pace and the Lord spoke to me: "Your ministry moves slowly in shallow water but watch what I will do with it when you're out in the deep." This came as a simple reminder that God had not forgotten me. Although I was in America serving another man's vision, I was on a journey to Africa and it wouldn't be long before the children's home dream came to pass.

There are many miracles I could tell you about from the Bay Revival, but the most precious one to me came when I found out that I was pregnant. I'd asked the Lord a few years earlier for a baby boy, and I promised that I would call him Josiah. Life was busy, manic and stressful, but the prospect of being parents was extremely exciting.

Chapter 9 – Birth pains

Back in Britain and preparing for the birth of baby Josiah, I was shocked when Nathan Morris sat me down and delivered what at the time I saw as devastating news. He believed that Shake The Nations and Shake The Nations One By One had reached the end of their journey together and that God had spoken to him to launch me into my own ministry. Nathan felt that he was holding me back and that the dream of running my own orphanage would never come to pass if I continued to serve him as I had been doing. He believed Matthew and I needed to stand on our own two feet and to oversee our own ministry. In fairness, Nathan said he would stand with us financially and offered to pay my salary for one year. He also made a substantial donation towards the children's home project, which had reached £10,000 through random gifts but still required a further £100,000.

If I'm honest, Nathan's words were tough to hear. Matthew and I loved Nathan with all of our hearts. We'd been with him from day one, on every crusade and almost all other meetings. We couldn't imagine ministry life without him, and with a baby on the way, we felt that we should focus on raising Josiah and wait for the appropriate time before being launched out on our own.

But we learned some pivotal truths during this difficult time – God's ways are above our ways, His timing might not always make natural sense but it's always perfect, and just because a situation might seem tough and bleak, it doesn't mean that God isn't in the driving seat. Nathan told me that just as I was about to give birth to Josiah, God was also going to birth in me my own ministry. It didn't make sense at the time, but I reluctantly accepted Nathan's proposal and One By One was launched as its own separate entity.

Running my own ministry made me feel extremely vulnerable. I didn't feel up to the task, I thought that Nathan's growing prominence would aid us and that had become my dependence, which of course was wrong. I also felt lonely, isolated and utterly inadequate. But as I've grown in ministry and read the Bible, I've learned that these feelings and emotions are normal for anyone who God has called. The Lord wants us to rely on Him and Him alone. He will remove safeguards, shortcuts and safety nets. He'll do anything He can to draw us closer to Him and into His presence.

If running a ministry on my own wasn't bad enough, what happened next seemed to make things worse. Josiah Matthew Murray entered the world on July 8, 2011, but the ecstasy of parenthood was quickly overshadowed with the sudden fear of death as Josiah struggled to feed in his first few days and it became apparent something major was wrong. He was rushed to a specialist hospital when he was four days old and emergency surgery was performed on his bowel. They warned us that the rare condition he had meant he might not survive and we spent the first 19 days of his precious life in hospital.

One By One was in its early stages and felt so fragile, but that wasn't my main concern at this time. My priority was little Josiah who was fighting for his life as doctors began to speak negative words over him and warn us of all potential consequences. One night I was stood at the end of his incubator while he was breathing through a life support machine, not knowing whether or not God would bring him through. We had no word from God or special prophecy to cling to, we simply had hope in a God who we knew cared.

I soon realised that being a Christian doesn't give us a golden ticket to a problem-free existence. In fact, many faithful believers go through horrendous hardships, far worse than we ever went through. I was reminded of Shadrack, Meshack and Abendigo who, in Daniel 3:17-18, said that even if God didn't deliver them from the fiery furnace, they wouldn't compromise and bow down to other gods. I loved God and trusted him. I had no idea if he would heal Josiah, but even if he didn't my trust would still be in His everlasting arms.

Josiah's ordeal lasted nine months, ironically the same time as we'd just spent in a worldwide healing revival. We didn't speak in one church during that time, so barely promoted One By One. We simply spent almost every hour God sent in hospital or at home caring for our ill baby boy. Josiah had five surgeries, and on the final one in April 2012, he was declared completely well by the doctor. What a relief!

One concern during this whole time was that the Kenya project appeared on pause, yet Pastor Gerald and the team on the ground in Bumala 'B had already began to lay the foundations of the building with the money we had sent and had identified children who might be suitable candidates to move into the home. As a result, Matthew and I made one of the hardest choices of our lives in November 2011. We decided to fly to Kenya to meet the children, leaving Josiah – who was still extremely sick and vulnerable – with Matthew's parents.

We spent a mere 48 hours in Kenya (That's a long way to go for a weekend!) but we managed to interview every child wanting to come into the home. We hired a professional social worker and began to weep as we read their reports. Words such as 'rape', 'torture' and 'abuse' were all too common on these documents. This was a matter of life and death. We couldn't fail these children. The gospel was their only hope and we were the ones who had been given the task of rescuing them.

It felt that the period from July 2011-April 2012 was the toughest time of our lives. We were attacked in almost every area imaginable and felt like we were in an intense spiritual battle. Looking back, although it was naturally the hardest period we've gone through, it was vitally important for our marriage, our family and for One By One. God was shaping our character, forcing us to trust in Him. It was hard but necessary.

The ethos of our ministry is based on John 4, where Jesus stops for a woman at a well. He takes time out of his busy schedule to spend time with this lady, and as a result, the entire region comes to Christ. If we would just learn to stop and help one person, there's no telling what God could do in our lives and in the lives of others. God took Matthew and I out of a popular healing revival and into a hospital room. To the outsider it seemed like we had vanished and our ministry had ended, but could it be that Almighty God was teaching us the vital principle of loving and stopping for the one through our own son Josiah? God certainly works in mysterious ways.

Chapter 10 – Bananas

Let me rewind to August 2010. Matthew, Nathan and I were at Starbucks in Daphne, Alabama, and were joined by our dear friend and mentor, Pastor Cleddie Keith. Pastor Cleddie had arranged the meeting at Church of His Presence which sparked the Bay Revival and was a long-term friend of Pastor Kilpatrick.

Once you meet Cleddie Keith, you won't forget him. Our paths crossed for the first time in 2007, and since then he has done nothing but bless, encourage and inspire One By One. His trademark phrase 'I believe in you' is more than a neat saying; it's a declaration from a man I'm proud to call my spiritual father. Pastor Cleddie has one of the most powerful prophetic giftings I've ever come across. I've been in services where he's called people to the front and told them their whole life story. On that hot afternoon in Starbucks, Pastor Cleddie told me he had a word for me: "Bananas!" We burst out laughing and thought he was joking. What was he talking about? He said nothing more, but just repeated the word: "Bananas, bananas, bananas!"

Although we're separated by the Atlantic Ocean, Matthew and I see Pastor Cleddie three or four times each year, and we're in regular contact on the phone. Two years went by and I was still none the wiser about the meaning of this 'bananas' prophecy, so I'd frequently probe Pastor Cleddie and laugh with him about it each time we met. He would simply respond by saying one day I'd know what it meant.

In May 2012, following Josiah's recovery, Matthew and I started speaking in churches. We'd managed to send some further funds to Kenya to help with the children's home, but were still more than £70,000 short. We had a few invites to speak at various churches in Britain and thought this would be a good opportunity to share our vision and to see if anyone wanted to join us in the project. We travelled to Kentucky, USA, in May to speak at Heritage Christian Fellowship, and the Lord spoke to a lady in the crowd to do a sponsored walk in aid of One By One. This was a wonderful gesture, although we assumed it might only raise a small amount like a few hundred pounds, as such events usually do. Still, every little helps, and we were grateful for her willingness to get behind the project.

A few months went by, and we received an e-mail from this lady saying that she had completed the walk and had in fact raised $19,000 (about £12,000). We were staggered. How could a sponsored walk raise so much? She revealed that one donor, a wealthy friend, had given $15,000 (about £9,500). This man was a complete stranger to us. He had never heard of me, Matthew or One By One, but he was touched by the vision when he heard about it and decided to give so generously.

We returned to Kentucky the following October and asked if we could meet the man and thank him for the kind gift. He agreed, and we were driven to his large house just outside Cincinnati. As we knocked on the door, we were greeted by an older gentleman in his early 90s. He invited us in and we spent a few hours talking together about our mutual love for Jesus and the work we had committed to in Kenya. As we were leaving, this man slipped another cheque in my hand, this time for $10,000 (about £6,250), and a few months later, he sent $30,000 (about £18,750) to the ministry. In less than a year, this man had donated $55,000 (about £35,000) to the project, and he has since become a regular supporter of One By One. We have an open invite to visit his home every time we're in town.

I don't feel it's wise to reveal his name, nor is he the type who would like any publicity, but I soon learned that he and his family are some of the wealthiest people in America. They have owned several high-profile businesses, sports stadiums and all kinds of properties and other ventures. In fact, one of his family members was at one time number 130 in the Forbes Rich List. As this man named some of the businesses that he had been involved in, one in particular grabbed my attention. He revealed that the family once owned one of the largest banana producers and distributors in the world. The company is a well-known brand that most people would have heard of. As we discovered this, we were reminded of Pastor Cleddie's prophetic message from 2010. God had been so wonderful. He had provided for His work – I guess you could say it was bananas!

Although the gentleman I've described made a sizeable donation, the remaining balance to fund King's Children's Home – the name we'd decided on for the orphanage – was provided in less spectacular circumstances. This pleased me though. If one wealthy businessman would have approached us and paid the entire bill, of course that would have been incredible, but that's rarely how God works. No faith would have been required, and without faith it's impossible to please God.

We learned a lot about trusting the Lord during this process, and gradually, we were amazed as eventually £110,000 had been donated to pay the bill in time for our planned opening in December 2012.

Every week something incredible would happen. A cheque would come through the post, a church would make a donation after hearing us speak, friends, family members and other individuals – some of whom were complete strangers – would commit to sponsoring a child. One businessman in America even sponsored ten children! We were seeing the provision of God. Of course we worked hard and did all we could, but there was no way we could have raised such a large sum of money in such a short time without divine intervention.

There is rarely a week goes by without One By One receiving a financial miracle. Christians across the world will write to us and say that God has spoken to them and they are to send a cheque. God has been so good to us.

The provision gave me confidence that the Lord was with us. We weren't even asking for money, yet people were sending it in. This had to be a move of the Holy Spirit.

I was reminded of the vision I had in Alabama where the fast-moving ship sailed past Mobile Bay. The Lord spoke to me that as we went through the deep waters, the ministry would pick up pace. Having gone through the heartbreak of almost losing our son, we were beginning to see God was fulfilling the second part of that prophecy…

Chapter 11 – Children of the King

Having spent every night of their lives sleeping on a floor, the initial 42 boys and girls at King's Children's Home were somewhat confused as I introduced them to a bed, a blanket and a pillow for the first time. It was a beautiful moment and revealed just how vital it was that we gave these beautiful babies a place they could call home.

The date 12/12/12 is one that will stay with me forever – the grand opening of King's Children's Home, Bumala 'B, Kenya. My good friends John and Caroline Wilkinson had flown in from Britain to hold a gospel crusade on the adjacent land, while Pastor Gerald and his team on the ground had been working tremendously hard to ensure everything was ready in preparation for the opening. I flew out with my sister Donna Shaw and my close friend Lindsey Everatt and spent three weeks in Kenya, the longest time I'd been away from Josiah, while Matthew flew in for a few days to join us for the opening ceremony.

Although the launch of the children's home provided one of the greatest joys of my life, I immediately realised that keeping it going was to be no small task. Raising funds to erect a building is one thing, but once it's open and complete, there are large monthly bills. One By One would be paying for every meal, item of clothing, education materials, building maintenance, not to mention the 17 staff we had to employ which included teachers, matrons, security men, cooks, cleaners and administrators. But the same God who had provided £110,000 to build the site wouldn't let us down. These are His children after all, He's just allowing us to play a small part in helping them along the way.

It wasn't just the financial pressure that was at times overwhelming – almost all of the children came to King's in extremely needy circumstances. What didn't help was a vicious rumour circulating around the village that I was indeed a white witch who had been sent by the devil to curse and kill the children. It sounds absurd, but such murmurings can be quite common in Africa, and with no credible newspapers or TV networks in the bush to quash these claims, you have to simply ignore any opposition and trust God to turn it around.

The great pioneering missionary to China Hudson Taylor shocked locals when he wore their clothes and spoke their language, and I determined to follow suit in Kenya. Although my Swahili is far from fluent and I can only speak the basics, I have tried to learn parts of Luhya too, which is the tribal language in Bumala 'B. Over time, this has helped bring down cultural barriers with the villagers and made them much more trusting of this supposed witch!

On meeting the children, I was instantly smitten, but knew that a lot of work had to be done. In some cases they were physically scarred, emotionally damaged and mentally affected. They would need lots of care and love, as well as the supernatural power of the Holy Spirit.

Nine-year-old Emmanuel Wesonga was one such case. His elder sister died and his father turned to alcohol, resulting in many violent arguments with Emmanuel's mother. One night they were arguing so a terrified Emmanuel hid in the cupboard to avoid the tension. When he eventually came out, his mother was so angry that she took it out on him and cut his head open with a machete – he still has a deep scar to this day. His father went out drinking and was eventually found drowned in a nearby lake. Emmanuel was left alone with his brother Seth and his mother, but she rarely fed them and refused to give them a normal childhood. Instead they were made to do household tasks in horrendous conditions. Eventually the mother had enough and walked out on both children, leaving them with the grandmother who was equally as nasty and abusive. Emmanuel was one of the first children we accepted at King's.

Eight-year-old Joan Agutu Orech has seen both her parents and all of her siblings die of HIV. She is also HIV positive and extremely ill. She has little energy and her teachers often report that she falls to sleep in lessons. We need God to do a miracle in her life. Mohammed Onyango, eight, was riddled with jiggers (a parasite that lives in dirt and eats away at flesh) in his hands and feet. His father had died and his mother is blind so couldn't look after him. Mohammed has struggled with his health, his studies and he couldn't even hold a pen in his hand due to the pain. My medical skills came in handy and I was able to bathe his feet during one of my visits and I taught the staff how to treat the jiggers in my absence.

These stories broke my heart. How could anyone not love these children? Although their past experiences would haunt some of them, I knew that through the power of God's love, we could see their lives turned around. I held job interviews that week and was confident we had employed good Christian workers to care for the children on a day-to-day basis. Of course the children needed good education, lifestyle and hygiene training and a healthy diet, but even more importantly than that, their primary concern was a lack of love. They had been abused and put through all kinds of torment, but I was determined that the love of Jesus would bring about change.

Chapter 12 – The power of love

I can only describe what has happened at King's Children's Home since it opened in December 2012 as a move of the Holy Spirit. It's difficult to know where to start, and these small pages don't really do justice to all God has done. The heartbreaking stories described in the previous chapter are now distant memories; the children beam with joy and you would never guess they had gone through so much abuse and torment.

Most of the boys and girls have given their lives to Christ, and I've had the privilege of baptising many of them in a local river. They worship with passion, they pray with fervency and they have started joining me on village evangelism, seeing people healed and set free by God's power. Each time I visit King's, the children run out to the car and scream with excitement and throw their arms around me. They're the most precious, beautiful, happy children in the world (yes, I know I'm a little biased!).

Little Emmanuel – who we mentioned previously – is a transformed boy. Although his physical scars where his mum beat him remain, he has experienced a wonderful emotional healing and he is now one of the happiest boys in the home. God has done a work in all the children. Whereas they were previously shy and terrified, they're now bold and ambitious. Some of them dream of being doctors, politicians and pilots; others want to pursue the ministry and become pastors and evangelists. We've also seen them perform well in our school and they're continuing to achieve good grades, a miracle in itself considering how late some of them were in starting any form of education.

Although we are rejoicing at what God has done in the 42 children we started with, we are still overwhelmed and frequently upset at other needy situations in and around the village. One case in particular sparked a whole new project for One By One, as a 14-year-old girl named Ann Adhiambo came to King's and asked if she could live in the home and attend our school. She said she was an orphan but the death certificate she produced was in fact counterfeit. So desperate for good education and regular meals, this girl's only hope was to lie about the death of her parents. I felt challenged to start a new work – we needed to create a structure for poor families to have their children educated, fed and raised in a Christian environment. We consequently launched our Homebase project, and now have 62 children who come to King's every morning for school and meals before returning to their families in an evening.

One girl who has joined the project is Daisy Atieno, who lives with her grandfather as both her mother and father have died. Daisy was abused as a baby and was once made to sit on an open fire as a form of punishment when she was just two. She has bad burns on her bottom, hands and face as a result of the abuse, and is clearly traumatised with what happened. She struggles to do simple tasks that other children can do and she is one of the girls we are praying God will heal.

We've also had one more addition to our original 42 as nine-year-old David Zakayo joined us permanently in December 2013. David's story is one of the most powerful I've come across. It all started when we went into the local medical centre to pray for the sick – a privilege we're now granted on each visit. In September 2013, I met a lady in the centre who was on her deathbed, suffering from malaria and typhoid. I prayed that God would heal her, but she remained sick and we were told she would die. I returned in December 2013 and was approached in the village by a woman, who asked if I recognised her. I had no idea who she was, but she revealed she was the lady who I'd prayed for a few months earlier. The very day after we had prayed for her, God had raised her up. She was completely healed and had no trace of sickness.

This lady had told everyone what had happened, and she'd also come to learn of King's Children's Home, and had been telling people in her village – a few miles from Bumala 'B – about our building and various projects. She said there was a little boy in her village who she'd like me to meet, so I agreed to go and see him. Having ridden a few minutes on a motorbike and then stumbled through bullrushes and dirt, I saw a lonely house separated from all the others. It was here I found little David. His mother had died of TB and was buried next to the house, and his father worked away as a security guard. I learned that for four years David had lived completely alone with no education. His house smelt damp and rotten, and he'd survived by eating grass, worms and the occasional meal from a generous neighbour. I looked into his eyes and saw emptiness, pain and loneliness. But this existence had become normal for David for many years. Normally I would never cry in front of a child, but I couldn't hold back the tears on this occasion. It broke my heart and I immediately knew I had to rescue him.

David agreed to join King's and we quickly had him checked at the medical centre. The first time I saw him smile was when he found out he was HIV negative. This summed up David's life so far. He moved into King's Children's Home on December 9, 2013, and has become a crucial part of the One By One family. Today David is a different child. He's happy, excited and friendly. He laughs, smiles and plays with the other children, who treat him like their own flesh and blood. What a glorious God we serve!

Another project we worked on throughout 2013 and 2014 was the building of a new church. The tin shack erected after that first Shake The Nations crusade in 2006 was still doing a job, but it was a totally inadequate building especially as the church, under the guidance of our newly-appointed pastor Bonventure, was growing at a fast rate. Each week new people were converting to Christ and the crowd couldn't fit into the building due to the packed attendances. On two of our previous visits people were seated on the grass outside listening in through the windows due to lack of space. We determined we would build Bumala 'B its own church, and just like God provided funds for the children's home, he did the same for this project, and £60,000 was quickly donated to build a fantastic structure with a balcony, beautiful stage and rooms for children's classes and administration offices. It is adjacent to King's and seats close to 800 people.

Our dear friend Pastor David Jones, from Royston Bethel Church, South Yorkshire, brought a team from his church in June 2014 to officially open the site and hold a conference inside. It was a celebratory and awesome occasion.

We also saw the village chief, Mr Peter Odele, give his life to Christ on that trip, and many others in the village have also now responded to the gospel. We know this is only the beginning, but with a big church building now up and running, there will be a great place for new converts to be discipled and call home.

Chapter 13 – Mother Bumala

"Mama Bumala, we're ready to give our lives to Christ," said Godfrey Makhatsa, whose family I'd been visiting on every trip for almost two years. That simple sentence pleased me greatly. Firstly, Godfrey and his wife Christine were devout Catholics and bowed down to worship Mary each day. I had consistently told them about Jesus and invited them to church but each time they had resisted, saying that although they respected me, Catholicism was their religion and they had no desire to convert to evangelical Christianity. On my trip to Kenya in June 2014, however, they changed their mind, saying they were now ready to commit their lives to Jesus. I led each of the family in the sinner's prayer, and we gave them all Bibles.

The other thing that thrilled me was that it was the first time I'd been referred to as 'Mama Bumala' –

this made me feel extremely emotional. It was proof that this British missionary previously dubbed the 'white witch' had finally been accepted into Bumala by her African brothers and sisters. No longer did they view me as an enemy, but God had united us and now we were like family.

I couldn't imagine ever loving a village like I love Bumala, but the vision of One By One is to expand throughout the world. In late 2013, we felt stirred in our spirits and believed God would open up to us a new nation, and Sri Lanka in particular was on our hearts. We had no connections there but God made a way.

We booked a flight to America and were visiting Pastor Cleddie Keith in Kentucky. Amazingly, on the same night we arrived, the pastor of the largest church in Sri Lanka, Vernon Perera, was also there. We connected immediately, shared our burden for the nation and by July 2014 we were visiting his church, ministering in the slum areas of Colombo and starting to offer scholarships to children into a top quality Christian school in Ja-ela.

Sri Lanka is much different to Kenya. The poverty isn't quite as extreme – at least in the parts of the country we have visited – but the persecution of Christians is horrendous. We met one seven-year-old boy named Yohan who was beaten by his school teacher because he refused to bow down to idols. He declared he was a Christian and the only God he worshipped was Jesus Christ. This abuse went on for months, and Yohan became mentally affected by the bullying. But he is now attending a Christian school and One By One is contributing to his fees and meals. Our heart is to further expand into Sri Lanka and reach some of the areas so badly affected by the brutal civil war.

Several years ago God gave me a vision of multiple villages throughout the world. I saw small homes for orphans, a school, a medical centre and a church. In the vision, a light from our village went out into the surrounding areas and other villages wanted what we had, which was the power and love of Jesus Christ. This will become the blueprint as we look to expand the work of One By One globally.

We don't know where the Lord will lead us next; we are simply listening to His voice and trying to be faithful with what He asks us to do. We are still a small ministry with an administration team that is mainly made up of volunteers. I must thank my husband Matthew, without him so much wouldn't be possible, while our American co-ordinator Chelsea Jones works tirelessly for One By One.

The ministry wouldn't exist in the USA if it hadn't been for her faithfulness.

I would also like to thank the many other volunteers and partners who have contributed to One By One. We are truly grateful for every prayer prayed and every penny received. Our heart is to continue to reach the lost, not just orphans but the marginalised, victims of human trafficking, widows, the homeless and anyone in need of the love of Jesus.

The vision is so simple – to stop for the one. We might not be able to change everyone's life, but we can make a small difference in individual lives, one by one.